D1172264

PARK CITY - DOGTOWN

Photography by
Juli-Anne Warll

Published by SnowPaw Enterprises
PO Box 504
Park City, UT 84060

Design and Layout by Katie Bedigian

ISBN 13: 978-0-615-34514-7
ISBN 10: 0-615-34514-X

This book is printed with Soy Based Inks
Printed in Hong Kong.

PRINTED WITH
SOY INK ™
Trademark of American Soybean Association

To Keesha

My first Park City dog
1993 - 2006

$\mathscr{T}$his is a book of dogs. Well, dogs and Park City, Utah. After many years of missing photography in my evolving list of hobbies, I got a camera in hand again, and decided to pick a photo project to work on. My love of dogs, Park City and photography made this an easy choice. Although, I quickly discovered quickly there wasn't anything actually easy about it.

My goal was to capture images of a variety of dogs, showcasing them, while also visually sharing many places in Park City as well.

Taking dogs I'd mostly never met, to places they are not familiar with and often early in the morning, leads to a lot of added energy and many distractions. After the first few shoots and wondering, how will I ever do this, a wise friend said, "One dog at a time, Jules. One dog at a time." After over ninety individual shoots, I hope you enjoy this collection of canine personalities as much as I enjoyed trying to capture "one dog at a time," with my camera.

INDEX

Mick

Story Behind My Name: I'm named after Mick Jagger. Always figured myself as sort of a rock star, so the name fits.
Breed: Labrador Retriever
Location: Sundance Ski Resort (but I live in Park City)
Guilty Pleasure: Tuna Sandwiches
Job: Avalanche Rescue Dog
Unique Fun Fact: I've been known to hang out with the rich and famous. Once I dug out actress Glenn Close during a snow-burial training scenario.
What Makes My Tail Wag: A foot of fresh powder and 4 am wake-up call for avalanche control work.

Name: Rozzi **Nickname:** Muppet, Roz Poz **Age:** 7 1/2 months

Rozzi

Story Behind My Name: The ski company Rossignol was the inspiration.
Breed: Golden-doodle
Location: Deer Valley Ponds
Favorite Pastime: Jumping on unsuspecting sleeping guests to wake them up.
Alter Ego: An animal from the muppets.
Infamous For: Dunking my entire head in the water bowl when I take a drink. Then running around and slopping water on everyone.

Jasper

Breed: Samoyed/Pyrenees/Polar Bear
Location: Under the Town Lift
Best Trick: I sit upright on my haunches like a circus bear. I get so relaxed like that I often just tip over backwards
Favorite Pastime: Chillin' out.... Literally! I love lying in anything cold, especially snow
Unique Fun Fact: I don't eat my dinner until I hear "Bon Appetit."
Most Embarrassing Moment: The time I tried being a "moose matador." I was out for a walk at night and my mom put a red blinking light on my collar since it was dark. A moose saw it and charged me!

Brutus

Story Behind My Name: I'm a brute by nature.
Breed: Schnauzer
Location: Miner's House – Rossi Hill Drive
Guilty Pleasure: Chicken drumsticks
What Makes My Tail Wag? I don't really have a tail.
Unique Fun Fact: I'm bilingual. I get all my commands in German.

Frank

Story Behind My Name: I'm named after Frank Pembleton, the coolest TV detective of all time, according to my dad.

Breed: International Dog of Mystery

Location: The Shoe Tree

Guilty Pleasure: Ball. My sole purpose is life is chasing balls. I hope you will throw them again, and again, and again.

What Makes My Tail Wag: Fetching

What Makes Me Drool: Balls. I'm mentally ill when it comes to fetching.

Best Trick: Tricks are for losers. I fetch.

Unique Fun Fact: I go to work with my dad at his shoe store and I haven't eaten a single shoe. That might be because I'm too busy FETCHING!

Name: Taazi's Afghan Star **Nickname:** Taazi **Age:** 5 months

Taazi

Story Behind My Name: Taazi is the ancient name for Afghan Hound. Afghan Star was a hit movie at the 2009 Sundance Film Festival, so I was named Taazi's Afghan Star.
Breed: Afghan Hound
Location: Aerie Drive
Favorite Pastime: Perching. I think I'm an exotic cat. I pose on the top of the couch.
Unique Fun Fact: It takes hours to brush out my fabulous coat. Call in advance so I can have my hairballs removed.
Alter Ego: Prince Abdulla.....sheer royalty.

Benson

The Story Behind My Name: I'm a proper English chap.
Breed: Old English Sheepdog
Location: Ski Fence on Norfolk
Guilty Pleasures: Pig Ears
Unique Fun Fact: I was born without a tail
Most Embarrassing Moment: Getting caught taking a bath in the neighbor's brand-new water feature

Name: Benson **Nickname:** Big Ben, Whitehead **Age:** 9

Guiness

Story Behind My Name: I'm brown and white, I look like the beer.
Breed: Bull Terrier and Bassett Hound
Location: Main Street Park City
Guilty Pleasures: I love sleeping in
Best Trick: I crawl.
Unique Fun Fact: I love to roll on my back after each meal.

Dash

The Story Behind My Name: I have a TON of energy! I dash all over the place, so that's why I was named Dash. My nickname? Because I'm trying to get into the trash.

Breed: Yellow Lab

Location: Top of aerial jumps – Olympic Sports Park

Guilty Pleasures: I hunt for mice and voles, and I eat them!

Favorite Pastime: Hunting mice, voles, and potguts.

Infamous For: Being clumsy and knocking everything over, including (but not limited to): kids, lamps and plants.

Popcorn

Story Behind My Name: My dad's name was Cornbread and we wanted to keep corn in the family lineage.

Breed: Hungarian Beer Hound and Great Pyrenees/Golden Retriever mix

Location: Town Lift Plaza

Unique Fun Fact: This is not my first brush with fame. I was featured in People Magazine in 2004 when they had me to pose for a photo shoot during the Sundance Film Festival.

Other Talents: I am capable of filling in as a small pony for children's parties.

Phil

Breed: French Bulldog
Location: The Trestle at the Marriott Pools.
Favorite Park City Hangout: US Ski Team head-
quarters. Don't tell the CEO!
Guilty pleasures: I run from space heater to
space heater on chilly mornings!
Alter Ego: a 96-pound Chocolate Lab who loves
to swim (Bulldogs sink). Good thing my name is
Phil and not Phelps.

Tookie

Story Behind My Name: I'm named after gangster Tookie Williams (early leader of the Crips). We were on death row the same week, but I lucked out and got a home the day I was supposed to be put down. Tookie Williams wasn't so lucky.

Breed: Catahoula

Location: The fire station

Unique Fun Fact: I used to work for FEMA's Urban Search & Rescue looking for humans under collapsed buildings.

Most Embarrassing Moment: Firefighters had to rescue me from an entrapment in a pipe under the Rail Trail.

Lulu

Breed: Miniature Schnoodle (Schnauzer & Poodle mix)
Location: Park Meadows
Unique Fun Fact: I've crossed the country by car eight times so, I've earned my wings flying. When I stay in motels, I do not make a sound. We use sign language so we don't disturb other guests.

13

Sancho

Story Behind My Name: Sancho Panza was Don Quixote's most beloved friend and also kept him sane.
Breed: Aussie Shepard / Human
Location: Park City Golf Course
Favorite Pastime: Soccer
Unique Fun Fact: I'm Canine Good Citizen trained (CSC) for public access.
Most Embarrassing Moment: I peed on a jacket at an outdoor market and mom had to pay for it.

Gizmo

Story Behind My Name: I look like the charac-
ter Gizmo from the movie Gremlins.
Breed: Shih Tzu-Lhasa Apso mix
Location: Zoom
Guilty Pleasures: Spaghetti with lots of sauce
Unique Fun Fact: I purr like a kitty when I'm
content.

Maggie

Breed: Golden Retriever
Location: Park Meadows
Guilty Pleasures: I eat anything; pickles, bananas, oranges, chocolate and apples
Best Trick: (besides my riding skills) I can balance treats on my nose then pop the treat up and catch it in mid-air.
Unique Fun Fact: I had a passion for riding after my first day on a motorcycle. I never jump out and I love it whether we are going 10 mph or 60!!

Wayne

Breed: He's a rare breed; a blend of Scotch and Norwegian
Unique Fun Fact: He was an airline pilot for years. Now retired, Maggie is his intrepid co-pilot on their motorcycle adventures.
Favorite Pastime: Cruisin' together with Maggie on the Honda, they've been riding for more than 10 years.
Wayne Says: "If I knew how many good looking women this dog on a motorcycle would attract, I would have started doing this when I was 20!"

Zoey

Breed: Shorkie (Shitzu and Yorkie mix)
Location: Park Meadows
Favorite pastime: Chasing the cat.
Most embarrassing moment: Mom and Dad snuck me into a fast-food restaurant once. I pooped on the bench.
Alter Ego: A big ferocious dog.

Murphy

Breed: Yellow lab
Location: The Sound Garden
Guilty Pleasures: Stealing the attention from my human baby brother. My baby brother is cute, but I try anything to steal his thunder.
What Makes Me Drool? Chasing every blowing leaf in sight! I'm a retriever to a fault.
What Makes My Tail Wag? Chasing snowballs down our hill after a fresh snowfall. I can dive up to 8 feet to catch them and slide down the hill.
Favorite Pastime: Flirting with the ladies on Main Street

Quinlan

Breed: Border Collie
Location: City Park in bloom
What Makes Me Drool? Fish skin, no meat at our house - poor doggie.
Alter Ego: Lassie. I'm incredibly loyal and always find my way home.
Most Embarrassing Behavior: I dig my nose in between visitors legs for a grand welcome.

Roxanne

Breed: Rhodesian Ridgeback
Location: The Ski Bridge, Old Town
The Story Behind My Name: The song by the Police
Unique Fun Fact: I eat corn on the cob like a person.
Most Embarrassing Moment: I ran away during my photo shoot!

Simone

Breed: Rhodesian Ridgeback
Guilty Pleasure: Peanut Butter
Best Trick: Crossing my paws
Infamous For: Having gender issues

Lilly

Breed: Bernese Mountain Dog
Location: Town Run at PCMR
Unique Fun Fact: People think I'm well trained!
Most Embarrassing Behavior: When I go looking for my owner and always end up at the "Alamo"
Often Seen: Lying in the middle of Empire Ave
Infamous For: Being a shameless lover

Chinook

Breed: Malamute
Location: Off Gambel Oak Trail
Guilty Pleasures: Sucking on my toy ducks like pacifiers.
Most Embarrassing Moment: Eating so much sand (it was covered with spilled pickled herring juice) that I had to go to the vet with an obstructed gut.
Infamous For: Howling like a lone wolf when I hear a siren.

E n z o

The Story Behind My Name: Named after Il Commendatore — Enzo Ferrari.
Breed: Malamute
Unique Fun Fact: I've developed a little patch of red fuzz in the middle of my otherwise black head. My parents sometimes call me "Mr. Testarossa," Italian for 'red head' and the name of a classic Ferrari road car.
Most Embarrassing Moment: Swallowing a baseball-sized squeaky toy whole at my photo shoot.

Name: Enzo **Nickname:** The Goose ('cause my howl sounds more like a goose honk) **Age:** 10 1/2 **Weighing In At:** 90 lbs
Name: Chinook **Nickname:** The Duck **Age:** 8 months **Weighing In At:** 70 lbs (one big puppy)

23

Name: Saffron (Saffy) **Nickname:** Safferdoodle, Saf **Age:**3 **Name:** Posy **Nickname:** Pos, Poser **Age:** 2 **Name:** Daisy **Nickname:** Daisy Duke **Age:**3

The Oddles

The Story Behind Our Names: We had to be named after flowers (according to our dad's ex wife, since her name was a flower name)

Breed: Oddles!! Saffy and Daisy are Golden Doodles. Posy is a Schnoodle (Schnauzer & Poodle)

Location: Eagle Chair Bullwheel – PCMR

Guilty Pleasures: Taking other dog's toys

Best Tricks: None; oh well

Unique Fun Fact: Saffy: I like to sit on people, all 85 lbs of me. Daisy: I like my space. I'm independent. Posy: I'm vocal. I like to announce our arrival everywhere. My piercing bark could probably be heard on Mars!

Otis

Breed: Cairn Terrier
Location: Old Miner's House on Deer Valley Drive
Infamous for: Making talkie sounds to get attention
Unique Fun Fact: I've logged over 60 cross-country flights. Always under the seat, and never a bark or complaint.

Sabor

Story Behind My Name: My mom worked in TV when she got me. She couldn't decide what to name me, so she put me on the news and let the viewers call in with suggestions. They decided to call me Saber, after a saber sword, due to my tail being all white. Knowing I was anything but common, mom changed up the spelling to be unique: Sabor.

Breed: Dalmatian

Location: McLeod Creek Trail

Guilty Pleasure: I'm a belly rub slut. I have no loyalty when it comes to treats and belly rubs.

Unique Fun Fact: When my mom came to pick me out, all my brothers and sisters were white — not a spot in sight! (Dalmatians aren't born with spots, we get them as we get older)... but I WAS born with them! Mom swears I stole all the spots in the womb for myself.

Esther

Story Behind My Name: I was named after a character in a Phish song. In the song, Esther was a freaky girl at the circus.
Breed: Spitz/Pomeranian
Location: Zoom
Favorite Pastime: Driving (well riding) with my head out the window
Unique Fun Fact: People always think I'm a fox!

Breed: Old English Sheepdog
Location: The White Barn
Guilty Pleasures: Super Chicken. He's my favorite toy. A chicken with a cape who makes sounds when he flies.
Unique Fun Fact: I sleep like a human with my head on the pillow.
Fun Stuff: when my hair gets too long I often walk into open cabinets and glass door.
Most Embarrassing Moment: I recently peed on a person who was sitting on the ground.

Baxter

Biggie

Breed: "Westie" West Highland Terrier
Location: Off the Rail Trail
Favorite Pastime: Sunbathing on the deck
Unique Fun Fact: I love wearing clothes! I think I'm a dog model, I guess. My favorite is my green varsity jacket and orange striped sweater.
Infamous for: French kissing people when they pick me up.

Nikko

Breed: Blue Heeler/Catahula
Location: Poison Creek Trail
Guilty Pleasures: Peanut Butter
Best Trick: I can answer questions about beer by barking.
Infamous For: Cleaning the kitchen counters (licking them clean!)

Name: Nikko **Nickname:** Hampster Pants **Age:** 7 or 8... who knows. Age is just a number

Koda

The Story Behind My Name: It means friend in Apache.
Breed: Norwegian Elkhound
Location: Explosives Building - Daly Canyon
Guilty Pleasures: People food
What Makes My Tail Wag: When my mommies come home.
What Makes Me Drool: Meat lovers pizza
Best Trick: If you give me a treat, I'll give you a high five.
Unique Fun Fact: I give endless kisses
Most Embarrassing Behavior: Using the cats litter box as my personal buffet.
Alter Ego: Mountain Goat, I can gracefully maneuver myself up or down a cliffside like no other.
Infamous for: Chasing Tail... the cats, that is.

Lila

Breed: Lab
Job: Avalanche Rescue Dog
Location: Silver Lake area - Deer Valley
Best Trick: I can find people buried in avalanches.
Unique Fun Fact: I LOVE tomatoes and carrots
Infamous For: My solo chairlift rides. I'm an independent girl!

Bailey

Breed: Boxer

Location: The White Barn

Infamous For: Eating anything left on the counter - loaves of bread, entire pizzas, even bags of sugar.

Best Trick: Playing dead. I drop to the floor and put my legs in the air when I hear the word "bang!"

Parley

Story Behind My Name: I was named after Parley's Canyon, where I was born.
Breed: Golden Retriever
Location: In a Silver Mining Cart
Favorite Pastimes: We both love playing in the deep snow. We kind of go crazy around it! When there is no snow we love chewing things to pieces.
Guilty Pleasures: Chewing on things I shouldn't and then pretending it was my brother, Parker, who did it.
Unique Fun Fact: I have a very complicated, ambivalent relationship with water. My DNA tells me to jump right in, but my gut tells me it's too scary.
Infamous For: I'm the social butterfly of Lower Norfolk.

Parker

Story Behind My Name: Named after this paradise we know as Park City
Breed: Golden Retriever
What Makes Me Drool? Females
Unique Fun Fact: Like a typical guy, I don't like to admit my need for affection (some even call me aloof!), but secretly I love to spoon and cuddle
Alter Ego: I'm a Sleep-a-holic. I'll happily sleep all day if given the chance
Infamous For: My sis has the social skills but I'm always complimented on my good looks

Boston

Story behind my name: My mom, a huge Yankees fan, lost a bet on a baseball game. The winner got to name me. She's just glad I wasn't called Fenway.
Breed: Great Dane/Lab/Long-legged deer
Location: The Farm Trail
Unique Fun Fact: I chatter my teeth when I'm nervous or scared.
Most Embarrassing Moment: I had DNA test done on me, it came back POODLE! Seriously!?

Sherlock

Breed: Sheltie
Location: Silver Star
What Makes My Tail Wag? Chirping of marmots
Best Trick: Bowing
Most embarrassing moment: Making amorous moves on one of our cats.

Name: Sherlock **Nickname:** Chucky (because I tend to get carsick and throw up in the car) **Age:** 4 **Weighing In At:** 15 lbs

Roxy&Mia

Story behind our names: Roxy: My owner's daughter passed away in 2004, she loved Roxy clothing. I was named in honor of her

MIA: (Missing In Action) I was found running along the highway and taken to a local shelter where my mom soon adopted me

Breed: Pug

Location: Miner's Hospital

Unique Fun Fact: Roxy can hike 5 miles and Mia 3....that's a lot for a little dog!

Rufus

Breed: Portuguese Water Dog
Location: Jordanelle Resevoir
Favorite Pastime: Wading in the water
Guilty Pleasures: Sushi
Best Trick: "Touchdown Ten." When my team scores a touchdown I give a "high 10" after a little cheer song. (Or maybe it's a double-pawed high 5?)
Unique Fun Fact: I love carrots and lettuce

Biggie

Breed: English Bulldog
Location: Spiro Tunnel
Guilty Pleasures: Anything and everything a well-behaved dog doesn't do
What Makes My "Stump" Wag: Kobe beef. (Hey, I have distinguished taste buds!)
Best Trick: I can watch an entire football game without moving
Alter Ego: Rapper

Kona Bean

The Story Behind my Name: The first night in my new home, I ran into the kitchen and ate a handful of Kona coffee beans. I was 'wired" for hours!

Breed: Chi-Foxy (Chihuahua & Fox Terrier) aka Taco Terrier

Location: Drilled Rock from Miner's Day – City Park area

Guilty Pleasures: I love to wear warm coats

Favorite Pastime: I lay across my Mom's shoulders when she drives

Best Trick: I play soccer with my paws, but I'm a small guy so I use a golfball. It's got to be pink.

Unique Fun Fact: I love to chase squirrels, even though they are as big as me.

Most Embarrassing Moment: I relieved myself on a baby carrier sitting on the ground. I got in big trouble because there was a baby in there!

Alter Ego: A 150 pound Great Dane

Infamous For: Watching T.V. Animal Planet is my favorite

Brandi

Breed: St. Bernard
Location: Top of Guardsman Pass
Guilty Pleasure: I can't help myself when it comes to entryway rugs... I eat them all... they're so tasty.
Most Embarrassing Behavior: Farting when someone picks me up, it happens every time!

Bandit

Breed: St. Bernard /Golden Retriever
Unique Fun Fact: I was rescued from Hurricane Katrina and brought to Colorado where I was adopted.
Alter Ego: Eeyore
Infamous For: Falling asleep while eating my dinner.

Kiko

The Story Behind My Name: Princess Kiko is the third wife of the 2nd son of the Japanese Emperor. Princess Kiko has given birth to the heir to the Chrysanthemum Throne of Japan. We rescued our "Princess Kiko" from a grim past. She climbed into the back seat of our truck to come to Park City and right into our hearts! We felt she deserved a new and regal name to mark her transition to a pampered member of our Park City family

Breed: Akita

Location: Iron Canyon

Guilty Pleasures: Chicken, Duck & Pig Jerky

What Makes me Drool? Fish

Favorite Pastime: Napping. A girls' got to get her beauty rest

Best Trick: My High Five

Boone

Breed: Weimaraner
Guilty Pleasures: PBR
Location: The plastic bottle ball outside Squatter's.
Unique Fun Fact: Why I'm so cool in front of the camera? Because I'm a pro. In 2007 I was featured in Men's Journal Magazine in an article called 'Park City Cool."
Infamous For: Nudging people in the crotch when greeting them.

Marlie

Breed: Australian Shepherd
Location: Jeremy Ranch
Guilty Pleasures: Shredding fuzzy slippers
What Makes Me Drool: Peanut butter treats
Favorite Pastime: I love to jump and catch snow, snowballs, shoveled snow…you name it. I'll jump up high and catch it!
Unique Fun Fact: I'm a therapy dog with Intermountain Therapy Animals.

Rudy

Story Behind My Name: My mom adopted me around Valentine's Day and the dark, eyeliner-like color around my eyes reminded her of Rudy Valentino in a sheik costume.
Breed: Pointer mix
Location: Highland Estates
Guilty Pleasures: Ice cream
Unique Fun Fact: I'm the star of an award-winning children's book.
Infamous For: Being an adoption failure and spending over three years in various shelters.

Djinn-Jur

Story Behind My Name: A grandchild in my family started calling me Ginger, but my mom wanted something with a little more character. She found out about this ancient mythological character that stood for mischief that was spelled: Djinn-jur. It fit!

Breed: Lhasa Apso

Location: Park Meadows

What Makes Me Drool? Chicken breast with a light tarragon flavor

Alter Ego: The genie in the bottle

Infamous For: I'm often indecisive. For instance, in the morning I can't make up my mind to get out of bed or not, so I'll just lay there until someone coaxes me out or I finally feel like it.

Name: Franklin Nickname: Mr. Franklin America Age: 4 1/2 Weighing in At: 98 lbs

Franklin

Breed: Poodle

Location: The Old Bike Barn on Crescent Tram

Unique Fun Fact: I like to dye my Mohawk different colors for special occasions.

Most Embarrassing Behavior: I've been known to not notice screen doors in my rush to get outside.

Infamous For: Lying in the middle of the street near my home in Old Town.

Added Note: I am the Doggie Don of Park City.

Charlie, Ivory & Deuce

Breed: English Golden Retrievers
Location: Spiro Mine Tunnel – Silver Star
Story Behind My Name: Deuce: I was named after a Harley-Davidson motorcycle called the the softail Deuce.
Jobs: Ivory and Deuce: We were both Avalanche Rescue dogs at PCMR back in the day. We can ride snowmobiles, snowcats and more!
Unique Fun Facts: Charlie: I was brought into my family to be a hunting dog. I do love chasing game birds, but when I catch them I just lick them.
Ivory: I won the Purina "Incredible Dog Challenge" in 2001.

Lucy

The story Behind My Name: "Lucy" means bringer of light

Breed: Rat Terrrier

Locations: Newpark and Tanger Outlet Center

Guilty Pleasure: I love snuggling under the covers

Favorite Pastime: Playing fetch

Best Trick: I do a mean twirl, and am working on a handstand

Unique Fun Fact: At Doggy Day Care, there was a stack of dog beds that had been freshly laundered. I jumped up on top and really enjoyed that vantage point, so at home I dragged two beds from two different rooms and put one on top of the other enjoying my "throne" at home.

Sophia

The Story Behind My Name: My Dad had wanted to name his new dog after Sophia Loren. He found me, wanted to adopt me then learned my name was already Sophie. It was meant to be!

Breed: Airedale

Location: Ontario Mine Building

Guilty Pleasures: I love McDonalds hash browns! But, you can tell by my girlish figure that I don't eat them often.

Unique Fun Fact: Sour cream on my dog food is a delicacy, and I always smack my lips after eating it

What Makes My Tail Wag? Snow! I'm often called "Snowphie" in the winter I love it so much.

Alter Ego: A mountain lion. I love to crouch in a hunting position, before greeting other dogs; then I jump up and rush at them!

Most Embarrassing Behavior: I'm afraid of going in the water. Ever since my paws broke through some ice one time I haven't had any interest in it.

The Newfies

Breed: All Big Beautiful Newfoundlands
Location: Near First Time Run - PCMR

OLIVER, FERGUSON, APOLLO & ATLAS:
Guilty Pleasures: We eat better than most humans; dining on elk, buffalo, venison and lots of veggie.
What Makes Us Drool? Everything!! We're Newfs!

Favorite Pastime: To swim, swim, swim **Most Embarrassing Behaviors:** We've been known to drool. In the cold weather, it looks like we have frozen tennis shoe laces wrapped around our heads.
Unique Fun Fact: Our breed is the strongest swimmers in the dog world.

KODIAK:
The Story Behind My Name: I look like a big brown bear
Guilty Pleasures: I love dumpster diving and sidewalk scavenging. I enjoy popcorn, melted butter and ice cream for me to clean off the pavement!
What Makes Me Drool? Poop pellets - rabbit, deer, elk and moose are my favorites. Crotch sniffing is also right up there on the drool scale.
Best Trick: I am an expert "Counter Surfer" and can steal food faster than you can say "Dogzilla!"
Unique Fun Fact: The sight of a marmot has caused me to pull my Mom off her feet, dragging her like a sled. It's not my fault she's not smart enough to let go of my lead.
Alter Ego: Fireworks, thunder and avalanche blasting make me want to be a lap dog.

Maxime

Story Behind My Name: Maxime is French for Maximus, derived from the Latin meaning "greatest." Le Crème was added -to make me sound even more French and note my color!

Breed: French Bulldog

Location: Main Street

What Makes Me Drool: My sweet Anna in season.

Best Trick: Really....with a face like mine, who needs tricks to get attention!

Unique Fun Fact: We're called "frog dogs" because of the way we lay on our backs, with our back legs splayed out.

Raz

The Story Behind My Name: Raz means to tease or heckle. Just ask my brother Obi!
Breed: Yorkshire Terrier/Dachshund/Tibetan Terrier
Location: Newpark
What Makes My Tail Wag? Playing with people's feet, and running from Obi
Alter Ego: Do Ewoks have a princess? If they do, that's me.

Obi

Story Behind My Name: I have the prowess and cunning of a Jedi Knight. I'm named after the stoic warrior, Obi Wan Kenobi.
Breed: Akita/Samoyed/Boxer/Jedi Knight
What Makes My Tail Wag: Ski touring and hiking
Unique Fun Fact: I hate getting my paws dirty
Most Embarrassing Moments: Raz likes to bite onto my tail when I wrestle with dogs my own size.

55

Tootsie Roll

Breed: Miniature Dachshund
Location: Lower Woodside
Guilty Pleasures: Snuggling in laundry fresh out of the dryer
Infamous For: Chasing the neighbor's big black lab back into his own yard
Most Embarrassing Behavior: Sometimes I get so excited I make a little puddle......ooops!

Boo

The Story Behind My Name: Because I'm wild and sweet
Breed: Aussie Shepard/Border Collie/Coyote
Location: Silver Star
Guilty Pleasures: Little mousies
Favorite Pastime: Hunting, hunting and more hunting
Best Trick: Opening the sliding screen door
Best Trick #2: I can wave "hello" with both paws

Teddy

Breed: Sheltie
Guilty Pleasure: Licking the shower floor after my people have gotten out
Favorite Pastime: Fence sparring with the dog next door
Unique Fun Fact: I write book reviews for the Friends of Animals newsletter

Bailey

The Story Behind My Name: My fur is the color of Bailey's Irish Cream and Irish names run in our pet family.

Spinner

The story behind my name: Spinner in German means crazy one, like me.
Breed: Lab Mix
Location: Deer Valley Ponds
What Makes me Drool? Man can I drool! Throw a ball for me and you'll never want to touch it again! It's a true spit ball. I literally foam at the mouth, I get so excited!
Unique Fun Fact: When I eat, I take all the food out of my bowl, and eat it from the floor nearby.
Infamous For: Taking walkabouts at will.

Finnigan

Breed: English Bulldog
Location: Park Ave and Main Street
Favorite Pastime: Snoring (which generally means sleeping too). Seriously, I can saw logs like a lumberjack!
Unique Fun Fact: I ran for mayor (against incumbent Dana Williams) in 2005 But I was soon disqualified since I wasn't a registered voter over 18 years old
Most Embarrassing Behavior: If you take my Frisbee, I will hunt you down and hump you, not letting go until you give it back!

Astro

The Story Behind My Name: I'm named after Astro from the Jetsons Hanna-Barbera cartoon

Breed: Harlequin Great Dane

Location: The Judge Mine & Machine shop - Daly Canyon

Guilty Pleasures: I love to eat fresh powder snow

What Makes My Tail Wag? Getting a massage

What Makes Me Drool? Pepperoni Pizza, especially the crusts

Unique Fun Fact: My nose completely pink when I was a puppy, now it's solid black

Favorite Pastime: Watching "The Dog Whisperer" in Bed

Infamous For: My other modeling stints; one photo shoot with Danny DeVito and another with Zach Braff for a 2004 issue of Entertainment Weekly

Ingabord

Breed: Borzoi
Location: off Lost Prospector Trail
Unique Fun Fact: I'm the breed in all those old British photos — paws hanging over the baby bassinet, forlorn eyes looking back over the shoulder. Borzoi's are Russian aristocrat dogs.
Alter Ego: A fur stole. I love to be wrapped high around people's necks.
Infamous For: Escaping. No laundry room or garage is secure enough. When you get home I'll be on the couch.

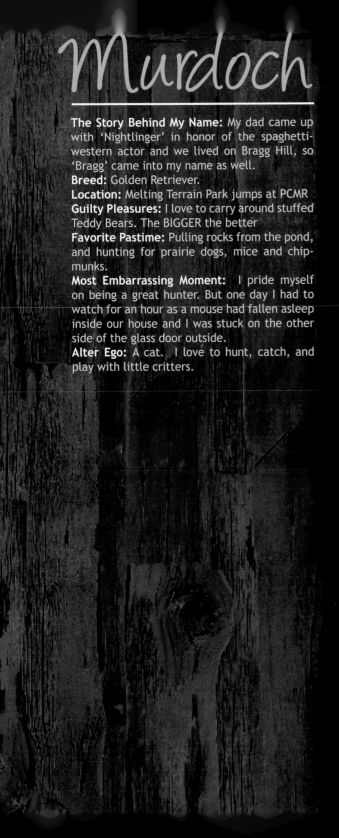

Murdoch

The Story Behind My Name: My dad came up with 'Nightlinger' in honor of the spaghetti-western actor and we lived on Bragg Hill, so 'Bragg' came into my name as well.

Breed: Golden Retriever.

Location: Melting Terrain Park jumps at PCMR

Guilty Pleasures: I love to carry around stuffed Teddy Bears. The BIGGER the better

Favorite Pastime: Pulling rocks from the pond, and hunting for prairie dogs, mice and chip-munks.

Most Embarrassing Moment: I pride myself on being a great hunter. But one day I had to watch for an hour as a mouse had fallen asleep inside our house and I was stuck on the other side of the glass door outside.

Alter Ego: A cat. I love to hunt, catch, and play with little critters.

Moonshine

The Story Behind The Name: My family started the first legal whiskey distillery in Utah..... need I say more?

Breed: Braque d'Auvergne

Location: The National Garage Building

Guilty Pleasures: The cat's litter box. I also have a penchant for the kids' superhero figures

Unique Fun Fact: Braque d'Auvergne is a breed of dog originating in the mountain area of France. My breed descends from ancient regional types of hunting dogs and are known to have been the dog bred for the Knights of Malta. As you can see, I'm a rare breed.

Most Embarrassing Moment: The day of my photo shoot, I gave the photographer a bloody nose and nearly a black eye! Last shot, I jumped off the whiskey barrel into the camera, smashing her in the face! So sorry!!

Alter Ego: Royalty. I'd like a throne.

Henna

Breed: Border Collie/Red Heeler
Location: The base of PC mountain
Guilty Pleasure: Stealing bones from the neighbor dog
Best Trick: I can flip when catching a ball
Unique Fun Fact: I rub against the furniture like a cat
Infamous for: Being true to my breed and nip-

Shiloh

Story behind my name: My predecessor, Cheyenne, was the same breed as me, but had super long legs. I look a lot like Cheyenne, but am much lower to the ground. So Chey Low... or Shiloh.

Breed: Blue Doberman Pincher
Location: The "Making Tracks" Sculpture
Best Trick: Catching Frisbees in flight
Infamous For: Running fast just for the fun of it!

Coco

The Story Behind My Name: I'm black with a white tuft of hair around my neck, just like the little black dress and white pearls made famous by Coco Chanel
Breed: Havanese
Location: The Marina at Jordanelle
Makes Me Drool: Parmigiano-Reggiano cheese
Guilty Pleasures: I love paper products and dryer sheets
Best Trick: Hopping like a bunny

Walter

The Story Behind My Name: I didn't exactly have a "proper" beginning, and I was given many other names, including Walnut. It was close but didn't quite fit. I finally ended up in a proper home with the very proper name, Walter. It fits!

Breed: Greater Wasatch Mountain Dog - Golden Retriever, German Shepard & Wolf mix

Location: The Trolley turn around- Top of Main

Guilty Pleasures: I have not control over myself when my parents leave butter on the table. I can swallow a whole stick of it in millisecond, then lay down innocently so they can't even imagine it was me who ate it.

Best Trick: I can talk. I say "I love you."

Unique Fun Fact: I'm an Intermountain Therapy dog, but my mom can't keep up with my grooming so I never get to go to work

Roshan

The Story Behind My Name: In Persian, Roshan means to enlighten or one who brings light
Breed: Shepherd mix
Location: Poppy Patch - Lower Deer Valley
Guilty Pleasures: Unstuffing my stuffed toys
What Makes Me Drool: Toy Poodles
Most Embarrassing Moment: Being chased by a pack of Chihuahuas
Alter Ego: Cleopatra

Duke

Story Behind My Name: Someone said "the Duke of Cool" in a Clint Eastwood film and it seemed like the greatest name.

Breed: Yellow Lab

Location: Freestyle jump platform

Alter Ego: A fox! I always chased them, but never could catch them. Even when I got close, I would just sit there and hang out with them. I even played with one once.

Added Note: Duke passed away shortly after this photo shoot. He lived the last couple years of his life as a three-legged dog, after being diagnosed with bone cancer. The vet amputated his leg and gave him just three months to live, but Duke lived another two years. Sadly, a new cancer formed and it was too much for Duke. His owners had him put down in their backyard, at that moment, two rainbows appeared in the sky.

Bandit

Breed: All Border Collie, baby

Diesel

Breed: Flat Coated Retriever
Location: The Easy Street Truck
Guilty Pleasures: I love toys and anything that squeaks...
What Makes Me Drool? Cheeseburgers
Unique Fun Fact: I'm a great swimmer. But, it wasn't always the case. Didn't start until I was almost 2 years old, and it didn't come naturally. I would struggle in the water, with my body upright. I was treading water and splashing more than swimming. Now I glide through the water with ease. So, it goes to show, you can teach a dog new tricks!
Alter Ego: The Nagger...I always press people to pet me, so whenever someone stops, I nudge their hand until they obey
Infamous For: When I get a new toy I always take it outside to introduce it to all of the other toys that fill my yard

Hercules

Breed: Maltese
Location: Silver Creek
Guilty Pleasures: BIG steak bones!
Best Trick: I roll over and present my paws to be cleaned if they are muddy
Unique Fun Fact: When I run, my back leg does a little "hop"

Sam & Bella

The Story Behind My Name: Bella means beautiful in Italian.

Breeds: Bella: Yorkie, Sam: Silky Terrier

Location: Main Street

Guilty Pleasures: Bella: I lay across my Mom's laptop so she can't work.

Unique Fun Fact: Bella: I'm a bit high strung, ok call me hyper. Sam: I'm the mellow one.

Brinkley

Breed: Bernese Mountain Dog
Location: Guardsman Pass
What Makes Me Drool: I LOVE Green Apples!
Unique Fun Fact: When my best buddies come over for a play date, I sit on their heads.

Lucy

The Story Behind My Name: My fur is the same shade of red as Lucille Ball's hair.
Breed: Irish Setter
Location: Off Prospect Trail
Best Trick: I bring in the newspaper every morning.
Most Embarrassing Moment: I was chasing a deer and the deer suddenly stopped and turned towards me. I ran in retreat and hid behind my Dad for protection.

Charlie

Breed: King Charles Cavalier
Location: Miner's Hospital
Guilty Pleasures: My toys, Mr. Blue Legs, and my new purple crab
What Makes My Tail Wag? I love watching Dogtown on TV (yes really)
Infamous For: I've had three surgeries on my eyes (my life was rough before my new life in Park City). Now I can see again and chase every chipmunk in sight. Oh yeah, and watch Dogtown...love it!

niko

Breed: Pomeranian
Location: Willow Creek Park
Most Embarrassing Moment: One summer a groomer suggested they give me a "Lion Cut." Which means I had just the hair around my face and neck, with the rest shaved. I looked like I didn't have any pants on.
Alter Ego: Houdini — the master of escape
Unique Fun Fact: Being a Pomeranian...everyone thinks I'm a girl dog... but, I try to show that I'm an Alpha male

Bear

Breed: Puggle (Pug and Beagle mix)
Location: Franz the Bear
Guilty Pleasures: I have a foot fetish. I love to steal socks, shoes and slippers
Best Trick: I can catch my tail
Alter Ego: Batman

Admiral

The Story Behind My Name: Admiral means a naval officer of the highest rank, and my breed is trained to rescue people at sea.

Breed: Newfoundland

Location: Off Moniter Drive

Guilty Pleasure: I'm a notorious cuddle monster!

Infamous For: A good retiree take down. The retired neighbors are terrified of me. Dad says sales of Depends have skyrocketed in the local markets.

Best Trick: After a "stay" command, I'm released by an officer's salute.

Butch

Breed: 1/2 Papillon 1/2 Coyote
Location: Glenwood Cemetery
Guilty pleasures: Eating grasshoppers
Unique fun fact: Crime-scene tape terrifies me
Good thing I'm not a police dog!

Auggie

Breed: English Springer Spaniel
Location: Lower Woodside
Guilty Pleasures: I'm a slightly nervous guy. I have to carry my favorite stuffed animals in my mouth almost all the time; pacifies me. My favorites are my stuffed animals; I can go find them all by name.
My Daily Mantra: I just want to love and be loved.

Infamous For: My incredible singing voice or my oral fixations; which extends to my attempts to rearrange the forest. I proudly carry everything from the largest logs I can manage on a hike. I often hit everybody on the trail in the back of the knees with my logs. Yeah, I'm that guy.
Best Trick: Carrying home cans and bottles I find on the trail to recycle.
Unique But Not So Fun Fact: I've had nine knee surgeries! On all of my legs but one. My Dad says, "It's not easy being Auggie!"

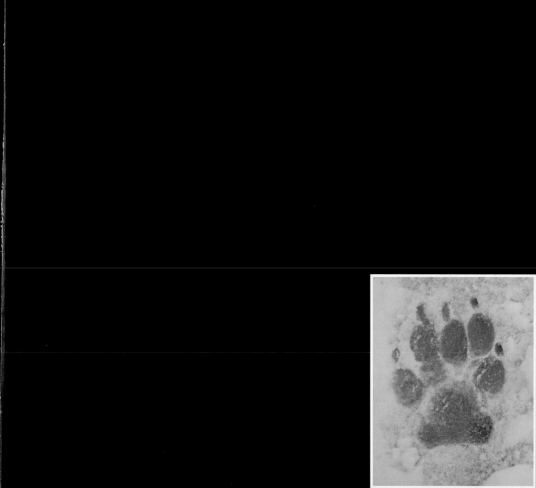

Mishaps and Adventures:

The end result of these photos may look like this was an easy project, and that dogs just easily cooperated in front of the camera. But that was hardly the case. With animals, you never know what to expect; suffice to say, multiple unplanned situations emerged. Let me share a few of the highlights with you:

- My gear bag getting peed on

- 3 runaway dogs (we got them all back): one through downtown and right past the view of the owners sitting in a coffee shop...wondering...was that our dog?

- One squeaky toy swallowed whole by a 90 lb puppy

-Being pulled off my feet and dragged on my stomach, camera in one hand and the other clutching to a dog collar. Silly me thinking I could actually stop a 180 lb. dog from running off

- A bloody nose and bruised eye after a dog jumped right into my camera lens

- 4 bites

- 1 completely camera shy dog (he didn't get in the book)

- 2 dogs freaked out by my assistant

-4 total posers

And many, many laughs!

We live
right about
here.

Thanks

A big thanks to all the wonderful dogs who got in front of my camera. Each was as unique and special as the Park City location they were photographed in. Thanks also to their owners for participating with their companions in this project.

A HUGE thanks to my amazing posse of lighting assistants: Packy Lennon, Rob (Frederick) Worthington and Will (Serge) Clark, whose help extended beyond lighting to dog handlers or chasers, gear valets, moral support and occasional sanity checks to said photographer. I couldn't have done this without your help, and your presence certainly added to the fun! Additional thanks to other friends who stepped in to help with the occasional shoot. Tommy Heinrich, your enduring positive encouragement all the way from Argentina sustained me through my doubtful moments of this project.

Editing help by Amy Roberts was welcomed and very appreciated. Additional thanks to both Dayna Stern and Bobbie Pyron for last minute proofing help. Katie Bedigan, your great design eye helped give shape to the project.

This is only a small representation of the many wonderful dogs around this town. I had to stop somewhere. My apologies to any dogs I couldn't get to this round. Fingers crossed for the next edition!

Juli-Anne has lived in Park City since 1992. Originally from Canada, she spent the bulk of her childhood in New Jersey. A love of the mountains and skiing eventually lead her to Park City. Photography has been part of her life since an early age. She played around with her father's camera gear and with his encouragement took photos everyday and spent hours each week in the darkroom. And her love for photography began.

After college, involvement in photography waned and her time and passion turned to flying airplanes. She flew as a commercial pilot for 12 years, but her creative side was repressed. The recent gift of an SLR digital camera rekindled the interest, leading to this project.

Juli-Anne currently lives in Old Town with her dog Jasper. This is her first book.